in association with

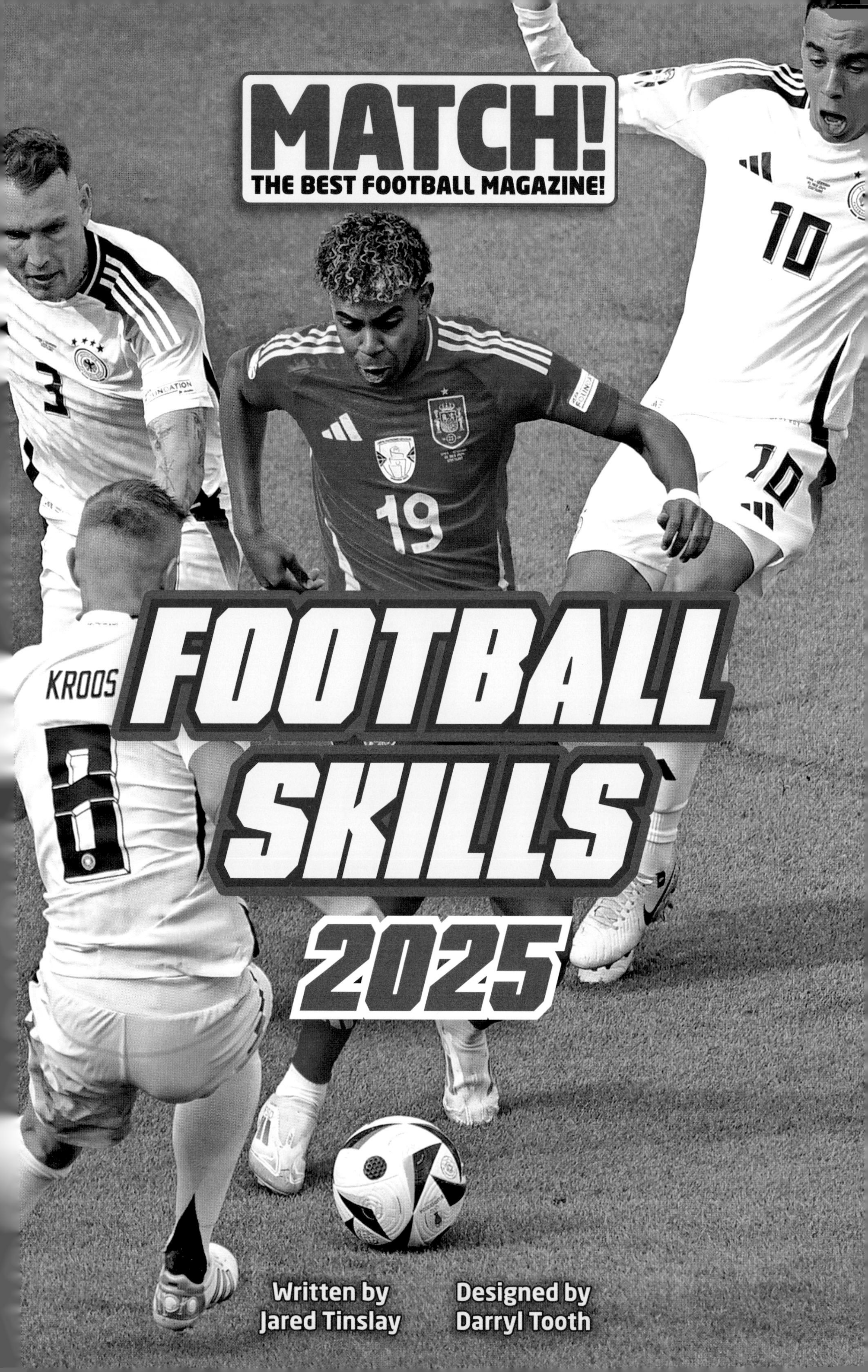

MATCH!
THE BEST FOOTBALL MAGAZINE!

FOOTBALL SKILLS

2025

Written by
Jared Tinslay

Designed by
Darryl Tooth

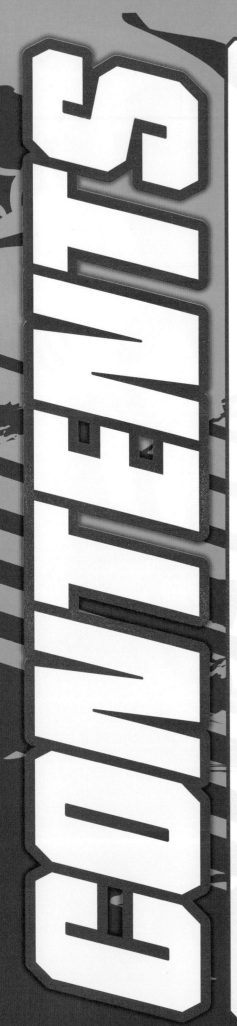

CONTENTS

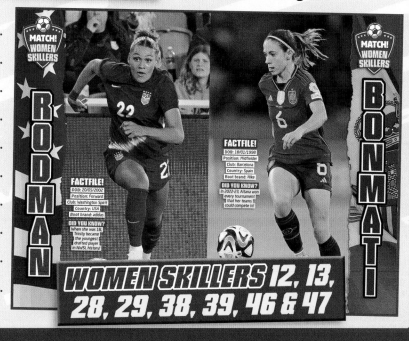

50
DEJAN KULUSEVSKI

Club: *Tottenham*
Country: *Sweden*
DOB: *25/04/2000*

James Maddison reckons the silkiest player in Spurs training is Manor Solomon, but all the winger's injury issues in 2024 meant our eyes have been on another target – Sweden star Kulusevski! "Deki" uses his super upper body strength to protect the ball and then sells his defender a sausage roll with, well... a body roll!

CONFIDENCE	DRIBBLING	TRICKS	AGILITY	WEAK FOOT
83	83	78	79	70

49
VALENTIN BARCO

Club: *Sevilla*
Country: *Argentina*
DOB: *23/07/2004*

MATCH hasn't been this excited about a left-back since former Real Madrid superstar Marcelo! "El Colo" signed for his first football club when he was just three years old, when most toddlers are still mastering the art of walking! He became known as a child prodigy in Argentina before moving to Brighton and then being loaned to Sevilla!

CONFIDENCE	DRIBBLING	TRICKS	AGILITY	WEAK FOOT
82	80	87	82	75

48
JUDE BELLINGHAM

Club: *Real Madrid*
Country: *England*
DOB: *29/06/2003*

Bellingham isn't what we would call an "out-and-out-skiller" as such, but he plays with the arrogance of one – a good kind of arrogance that all the world's top players need! Every time the young gun steps out onto the field, confidence totally oozes from him – and it often rubs off onto his team-mates!

TOP SKILL!
THE STEPOVER

CONFIDENCE	DRIBBLING	TRICKS	AGILITY	WEAK FOOT
90	85	80	79	82

47
ANTONIO NUSA

Club: *RB Leipzig*
Country: *Norway*
DOB: 17/04/2005

Defenders try to double up when defending Nusa, but sometimes you need more than two to stop the nippy Norway winger! The most dangerous thing about him is that he can take the ball on the inside or the outside, as he's not afraid to use either foot, which makes him mega unpredictable!

TOP SKILL!
THE NUTMEG

CONFIDENCE	DRIBBLING	TRICKS	AGILITY	WEAK FOOT
81	86	85	84	80

46
GABRIEL JESUS

Club: *Arsenal*
Country: *Brazil*
DOB: 03/04/1997

The Brazil baller said that his telephone celebration is a tribute to his mum, but we reckon he's actually got a hotline to legendary countryman Ronaldinho – because some of the skills he produces have that same Samba sauce! He always plays with a smile on his face like Ronaldinho used to as well!

CONFIDENCE	DRIBBLING	TRICKS	AGILITY	WEAK FOOT
84	86	85	90	74

45
ALEJANDRO GARNACHO

Club: *Man. United*
Country: *Argentina*
DOB: 01/07/2004

If there were individual awards for the year's most outrageous piece of skill, Garnacho's jaw-dropping overhead kick goal against Everton at Goodison Park would have won 2023's prize hands down! That took an elite level of technique and will go down as arguably the greatest goal in Premier League history!

CONFIDENCE	DRIBBLING	TRICKS	AGILITY	WEAK FOOT
85	85	83	88	80

44
SAID BENRAHMA

Club: *Lyon*
Country: *Algeria*
DOB: *10/08/1995*

The Algeria ace is one of the trickiest footballers on the planet on his day, but he's been on a bit of a drop ride in recent years – and not the sort you'd happily spend an hour in a queue for at an attraction park! His fall in confidence has seen him plummet from 26th spot in our 2023 countdown down into the 40s this time around!

CONFIDENCE	DRIBBLING	TRICKS	AGILITY	WEAK FOOT
80	83	90	85	83

43
CRISTIANO RONALDO

Club: *Al Nassr*
Country: *Portugal*
DOB: *05/02/1985*

The Saudi Pro League is absolutely on the rise, but the ageing CR7 is still a cheat code against that level of opposition! There are some serious showreels of his skills on YouTube since joining Al Nassr, including Elasticos, triple stepovers and nutmegs. Chill, Cristiano!

CONFIDENCE	DRIBBLING	TRICKS	AGILITY	WEAK FOOT
95	79	87	73	88

42
COLE PALMER

Club: *Chelsea*
Country: *England*
DOB: *06/05/2002*

"Cold" Palmer has ice in his veins - his Panenka penalty against Burnley in April 2024 was proof of that! In fact, we reckon his Chelsea team-mates don't even need to bother having ice baths after matches - they just need to spend five minutes standing next to the "Iceman" for the same effect!

CONFIDENCE	DRIBBLING	TRICKS	AGILITY	WEAK FOOT
90	86	82	90	75

41
ROONY BARDGHJI

Club: *Copenhagen*
Country: *Sweden*
DOB: *15/11/2005*

MATCH loves scouting under-the-radar stars from outside Europe's top five leagues - and Bardghji was one of our faves to watch in 2023-24, alongside fellow Sweden talent Lucas Bergvall! Roony bagged the winner v Man. United in the 2023-24 Champions League group stage, but sustained a serious knee injury in May 2024. Gutted!

CONFIDENCE	DRIBBLING	TRICKS	AGILITY	WEAK FOOT
85	86	88	84	81

40
ENDRICK

CONFIDENCE
88

DRIBBLING
87

TRICKS
85

AGILITY
87

WEAK FOOT
77

Club: *Real Madrid*
Country: *Brazil*
DOB: *21/07/2006*

After his unforgettable debut goal at Wembley in Brazil's friendly win v England in March 2024, European footy fans finally got to see Endrick's dazzling displays in the flesh after hearing about all the hype from Brazil! Now we get to see him busting out his tricks every week for Real Madrid!

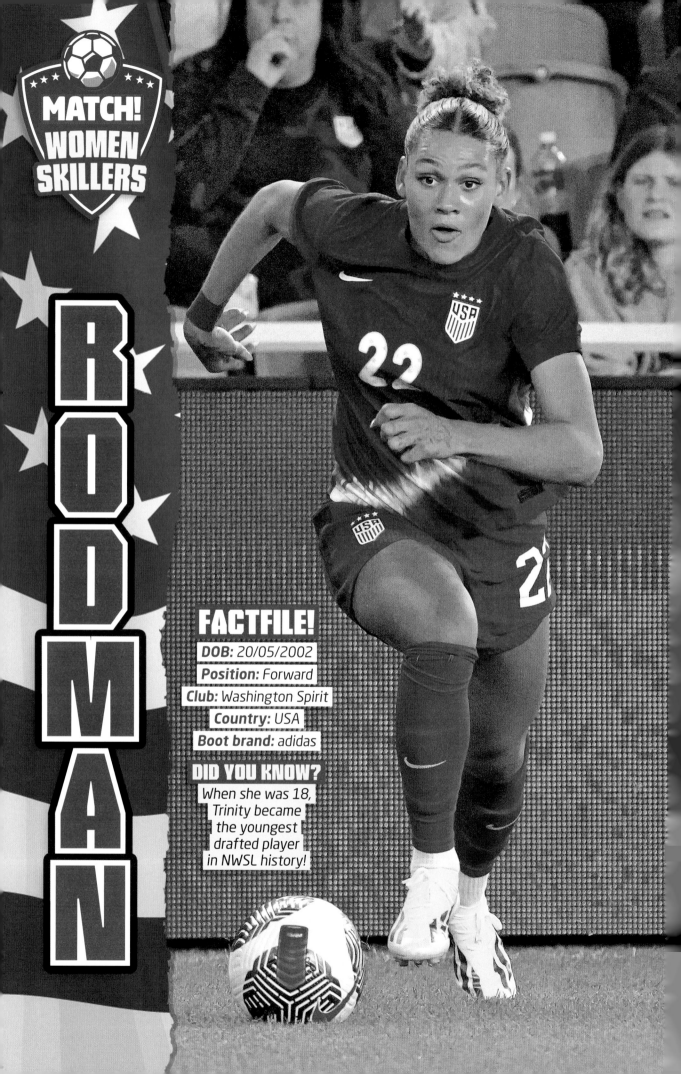

RODMAN

FACTFILE!

DOB: 20/05/2002

Position: Forward

Club: Washington Spirit

Country: USA

Boot brand: adidas

DID YOU KNOW?

When she was 18, Trinity became the youngest drafted player in NWSL history!

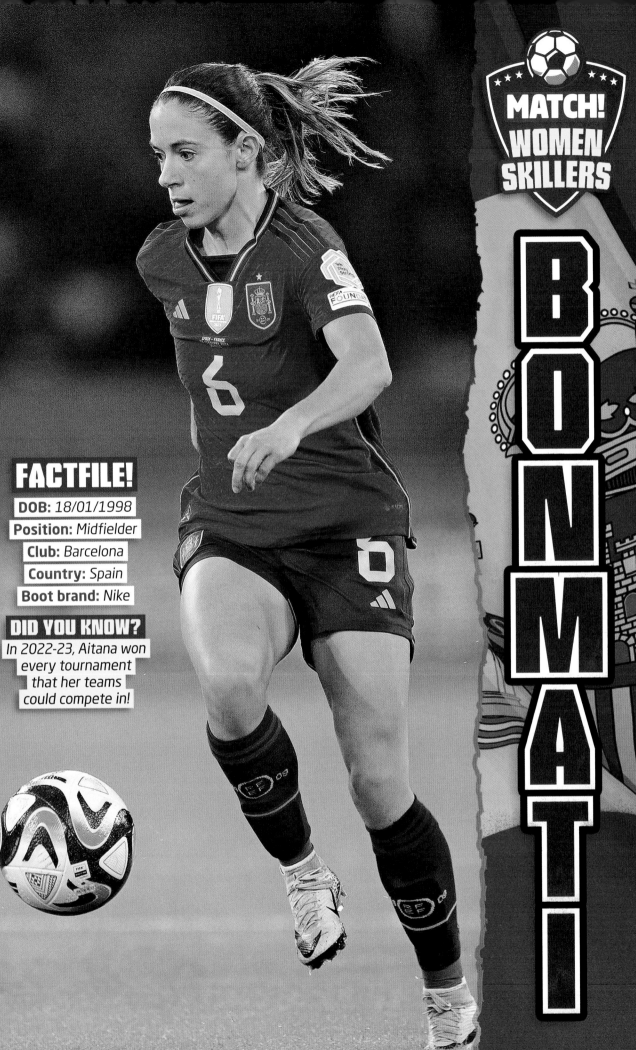

FACTFILE!

DOB: *18/01/1998*
Position: *Midfielder*
Club: *Barcelona*
Country: *Spain*
Boot brand: *Nike*

DID YOU KNOW?

In 2022-23, Aitana won every tournament that her teams could compete in!

BONMATI

SKILLS ICON NO.1
CRUYFF

FACTPACK!

Full Name: *Hendrik Johannes Cruijff*

DOB: *25/04/1947*

Height: *5ft 10in*

Country: *Netherlands*

Caps: *48*

Goals: *33*

Johan Cruyff was born and raised in Amsterdam, growing up five minutes down the road from Ajax's stadium! Little did he know, when joining their academy on his tenth birthday, that he would later have a stadium named after him in the southeast side of the city - where the club still play their home games today. He was an incredibly silky footballer and a key figure of the Dutch Total Football style - both as a player and a coach. The three-time Ballon d'Or winner is also one of the few players to have a skill move named after him!

CAREER LEAGUE STATS

Date	Club	Games	Goals
1964-1973	Ajax	245	193
1973-1978	Barcelona	143	48
1979	Los Angeles Aztecs	22	14
1980	Washington Diplomats	24	10
1981	Levante	10	2
1981	Washington Diplomats	5	2
1981-1983	Ajax	36	14
1983-1984	Feyenoord	33	11

DID YOU KNOW?

BARCELONA ALSO HAVE THEIR OWN JOHAN CRUYFF STADIUM, WHERE THE CLUB'S WOMEN AND ACADEMY PLAY THEIR MATCHES!

TOP SKILL!
THE CRUYFF TURN

CONFIDENCE
98

DRIBBLING
94

TRICKS
96

AGILITY
92

WEAK FOOT
95

SHOWREEL!

Scan the QR code to watch some of his best bits!

39

MICHAEL OLISE

TOP SKILL!
THE CRUYFF TURN

Club: *Bayern Munich*
Country: *France*
DOB: *12/12/2001*

Olise is one of those players who just makes football look easy! Even if a team-mate were to pelt a five-yard pass at him at the speed of light, he'd still be able to control it and then probably just shrug his shoulders and say, "Try harder next time". The silky France star has got that "va-va-voom"!

CONFIDENCE
86

DRIBBLING
86

TRICKS
82

AGILITY
93

WEAK FOOT
77

38

BERNARDO SILVA

Club: *Man. City*
Country: *Portugal*
DOB: *10/08/1994*

When comparing footballers to animals or insects, you'd think they'd probably love to be a lion or a jaguar, but we'd probably compare Bernardo to a worm – in the nicest way possible! He has that ability to wriggle his way past defenders and clearly excels in wet weather… ahem, Manchester!

CONFIDENCE	DRIBBLING	TRICKS	AGILITY	WEAK FOOT
90	87	84	93	73

37

PEDRO NETO

Club: *Chelsea*
Country: *Portugal*
DOB: *09/03/2000*

Wolves could have formed a ridiculously silky five-a-side team in 2023-24, with the likes of futsal lover Max Kilman, left-wing wizard Rayan Ait-Nouri, dribble king Matheus Cunha and the rapid Neto! The Portugal winger has always had bags of ability – he just needs to stay injury-free!

CONFIDENCE	DRIBBLING	TRICKS	AGILITY	WEAK FOOT
87	87	82	89	81

36

EBERECHI EZE

TOP SKILL!
THE BODY FEINT

Club: *Crystal Palace*
Country: *England*
DOB: *29/06/1998*

Back in 2020, Crystal Palace had to make a video with Eze explaining how to pronounce his name, because people kept saying "Easy"! To be honest, that would suit him to a tee, because he makes mind-boggling skills look simple! Maybe we should start a petition to pronounce it wrongly again!

CONFIDENCE	DRIBBLING	TRICKS	AGILITY	WEAK FOOT
90	88	83	85	79

35

XAVI SIMONS

Club: RB Leipzig
Country: Netherlands
DOB: 21/04/2003

An important part of life is being able to accept your mistakes - just ask PSG chiefs! They let Simons leave permanently in 2022 to join PSV, only to watch him tear the place apart with countless goals and assists. They still think he has mad potential, but have let him fulfil that on loan at RB Leipzig in Germany!

CONFIDENCE	DRIBBLING	TRICKS	AGILITY	WEAK FOOT
83	86	82	90	84

34

BUKAYO SAKA

Club: Arsenal
Country: England
DOB: 05/09/2001

Sometimes when we're watching the Gunners superstar, we wish we could add the slow-motion filter to the television! His feet move at such sensational speed that we have to keep rewinding to see how he beat his man in the first place. Help us out here, Bukayo!

CONFIDENCE	DRIBBLING	TRICKS	AGILITY	WEAK FOOT
91	95	80	87	72

33

MEMPHIS DEPAY

TOP SKILL!
THE SOMBRERO

Club: Free agent
Country: Netherlands
DOB: 13/02/1994

Every year, Memphis finds himself a few spaces further down this list, but that's only because his agility and dribbling stats are dropping slightly - he's still an elite trick machine! We saw him pull off a Sombrero flick over a defender's head in a league game as recently as March 2024!

CONFIDENCE	DRIBBLING	TRICKS	AGILITY	WEAK FOOT
87	86	94	81	78

32
PHIL FODEN

Club: Man. City
Country: England
DOB: 28/05/2000

MATCH has created a new adjective, which can be defined as "a combination of technical brilliance, jaw-dropping skills and thrilling flair"... AKA, "Fodenesque!" His unbelievable 2023-24 campaign was the best of his career so far, outperforming the likes of Erling Haaland and Kevin De Bruyne in a Man. City shirt!

CONFIDENCE	DRIBBLING	TRICKS	AGILITY	WEAK FOOT
89	88	85	91	74

31
SAMUEL CHUKWUEZE

Club: Milan
Country: Nigeria
DOB: 22/05/1999

MATCH is setting Samu some homework this year, and depending on how it goes he'll either be higher or lower on this list next year...and that's to work on his right foot! He has the dribbling, tricks and agility to be way higher up this list but he relies too much on his left foot, which makes him easier to defend against!

CONFIDENCE	DRIBBLING	TRICKS	AGILITY	WEAK FOOT
87	90	94	86	70

30
JADON SANCHO

Club: Chelsea
Country: England
DOB: 25/03/2000

It's a crying shame that Sancho felt he needed to leave Man. United to get his career back on track, but actually we're glad he decided to do something about it! There was far too much talent going to waste when he was bench-warming at Old Trafford!

CONFIDENCE	DRIBBLING	TRICKS	AGILITY	WEAK FOOT
77	89	94	89	79

WORDSEARCH

Find 30 of the Premier League's best-ever skillers in this grid!

```
H O T F                                              R H E N
Z M I Q                                              L T S F
B U D P                                              G M V C
Y M V M                                              C B P K
E F M A                                              E O F S
H V K K T P I U M O G U M T J F V F R B X R T N M N D F A X
X R A G Y Q K F X P O O R B A I I B J R D B H E D Y E Z K Q
W B R R K D B O E Z W W O J B R H T J L W Q A J C A R F Z B
W N V E D X M Y V X H M B H F M Y F T O G O P S K E K A B H
M W R B E D X P R J C V B E R I Q X V R D B A R T U A H Q I
M P Z Y K S S R Y T E I E H S N S X Q I J A O L M F D C M V
E U D B P Z V V Y B G Y N N P J O Z K C Y O J F D O I X O Y F
P W S E G S M O N J I O I X H D Z A K Y D H X L J Z Z K G H
W K K R H X A V H A Z A X I J C N V X I K K Y E H A K O U U
P Q E B A C A M P B T H U W U I M A R B Q R S T Q Y O T L K
O Y U A T D L J C W M F O A O V S N T L E L U I F D P P B A
H G M T K T O P E Z R X T I Z X I O B B K E Q S A M R Q U V
Z W M O A V N X U N N C Y Z L G N T A G T E Y S P J H O N G
Z S J V C T I Q G T P J P K P J J N R S F S N I G G B A E E
Y E T Z Y R G E B X V A R R M E G A A R N N R E L V W V W S
N C R C G H D G Q V U F C T O G G C A B O K X R C B D A V M
D C Y H N V C K S E L U R W L J J D T S Q N X E U D K C L L
P A Q X A B U B V Y B L D C B Z K P O F Y O A N H R Q L O I
S I H S E M A Z Z E I J Q X C F E L Y T X R I L S U B U H L
D R A Z A H M B X X O V R D D S P U T Y P R N E D D A H N D
V L U K T R J K K N E Q T U O I W H G A R H P E N O H K I I
O R G X F X V T T K D K S C T S I S B N N Q E X H A A O N L
N P E N O K O U E A B Q I K A A Z R B A I K S R Q Q Z Z U R
U K D O O K A N Y M Y P L P G J G F N Q N M I N K E H C J T
U I M S O X V U A I X M V O J O B I T A I T O J F U T N U J
I C E P I U Z T P P A Q A Z J T X L C A P O A D K E R F U P
E O A F M Z G M K V V F Y E A D B N E X A E M U O B G M L Q
N N S V W S I F F O P A C B J F W J C N Z L T L U A B Q Y L
G U Q T E P P W G R Y R J E Y N K O P B P V G A F P S I D J
I Z I I B N N P X I Q U Q L C Y N K S A I N T M A X I M I N
O K V V T R S G R H N C V W N G M Q R K X V Y S N Z L C U B
C N F A U L A U L L V W V S G F K E Y N P T D L S E G G S D
S B E N A R F A V Z A J P B Q K Q U N L I D D X U E Y I F P
A G C K M U B Q N N W R R Q M D F O N F D R W O I O H D N G
G G B O L A S I E J A B Q O P Z S X E L O C Z L I O V Y J Q
```

Ben Arfa, Berbatov, Bergkamp, Bolasie, Cantona, Cole, Di Canio, Djorkaeff, Dominguez, Firmino, Gascoigne, Ginola, Hazard, Henry, Juninho, Le Tissier, Lua Lua, Mahrez, Nani, Okocha, Payet, Robben, Ronaldo, Saint-Maximin, Silva, Taarabt, Thiago, Zaha, Ziyech, Zola

FOOTY MIS-MATCH

Study these snaps of legendary skiller Zinedine Zidane, then try to find the ten differences!

ANSWERS ON PAGE 60

RONALDO

Ronaldo Nazario is widely recognised as one of the greatest goalscorers in history - and his record speaks for itself - but he was also an incredibly skilful footballer! He famously said that futsal will always be his "first love", which he played on the streets of Rio de Janeiro as a child before moving on to 11-a-side. It was on those Rio roads where he nurtured the skills that would later see him break the world transfer record twice, win the World Cup Golden Boot and become nicknamed O Fenomeno - or, The Phenomenon!

FACTPACK!

Full Name: *Ronaldo Luis Nazario de Lima*

DOB: *18/09/1976*

Height: *6ft*

Country: *Brazil*

Caps: *98*

Goals: *62*

TOP SKILL!
THE STEPOVER

DID YOU KNOW?
HE'S THE ONLY PLAYER TO HAVE SCORED FOR BOTH REAL MADRID AND BARCELONA IN EL CLASICO, AND BOTH INTER AND MILAN IN THE DERBY DELLA MADONNINA!

CONFIDENCE 99

DRIBBLING 97

TRICKS 98

AGILITY 90

WEAK FOOT 95

CAREER LEAGUE STATS

Date	Club	Games	Goals
1993-1994	Cruzeiro	34	34
1994-1996	PSV	46	42
1996-1997	Barcelona	37	34
1997-2002	Inter	68	49
2002-2007	Real Madrid	127	83
2007-2008	Milan	20	9
2009-2011	Corinthians	52	29

SHOWREEL!

Scan the QR code to watch some of his best bits!

29
CHRISTOPHER NKUNKU

Club: *Chelsea*
Country: *France*
DOB: 14/11/1997

Nkunku turned down Chelsea's supposedly "cursed" No.9 shirt when he joined in summer 2023, but he still got mega unlucky with injuries during 2023-24, meaning fans of the Premier League barely got to see him ball! Providing he gets more minutes over the next year, we reckon he could shoot up the skiller rankings!

CONFIDENCE	DRIBBLING	TRICKS	AGILITY	WEAK FOOT
83	88	90	89	79

28
LAMINE YAMAL

Club: *Barcelona*
Country: *Spain*
DOB: 13/07/2007

Yamal landed a mega deal with adidas in early 2024 to wear their speed silo X Crazyfast boots, which actually first launched as the F50 back in 2004! That means the Barcelona and Spain wonderkid is actually younger than the boots he wears, although not the modern version of them...obviously!

CONFIDENCE	DRIBBLING	TRICKS	AGILITY	WEAK FOOT
89	85	88	88	80

27
KINGSLEY COMAN

TOP SKILL!
THE HEEL TO BALL ROLL

Club: *Bayern Munich*
Country: *France*
DOB: 13/06/1996

What do you get when you mix mind-bending speed with show-stopping skills? Kingsley Coman is the answer! The 2023-24 campaign must have been a bizarre feeling for the Bayern baller, who failed to win a league title for the first time in 12 seasons - and for the first time in his senior career. Mad!

CONFIDENCE	DRIBBLING	TRICKS	AGILITY	WEAK FOOT
85	88	91	92	73

26
LEROY SANE

TOP SKILL!
THE FAKE SHOT

Club: *Bayern Munich*
Country: *Germany*
DOB: *11/01/1996*

The flying Germany winger's main craft is using his pace to weave between defenders! In fact, we reckon he'll be hired to weave baskets once he retires from football! Hopefully that's still a long time coming, though – he had a sizzling 2023-24 season, recording his best-ever campaign in the Bundesliga for goals and assists combined. Legend!

CONFIDENCE	DRIBBLING	TRICKS	AGILITY	WEAK FOOT
93	88	89	88	72

25
MARCUS RASHFORD

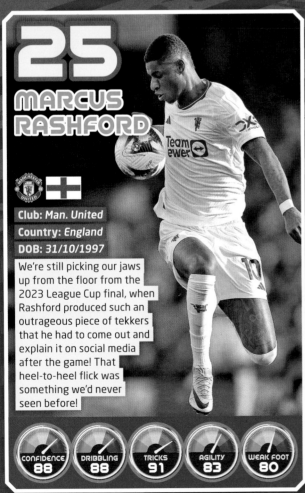

Club: *Man. United*
Country: *England*
DOB: *31/10/1997*

We're still picking our jaws up from the floor from the 2023 League Cup final, when Rashford produced such an outrageous piece of tekkers that he had to come out and explain it on social media after the game! That heel-to-heel flick was something we'd never seen before!

CONFIDENCE	DRIBBLING	TRICKS	AGILITY	WEAK FOOT
88	88	91	83	80

24
MARTIN ODEGAARD

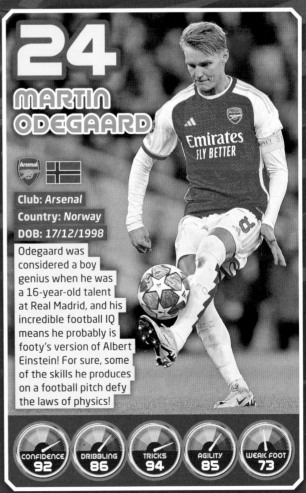

Club: *Arsenal*
Country: *Norway*
DOB: *17/12/1998*

Odegaard was considered a boy genius when he was a 16-year-old talent at Real Madrid, and his incredible football IQ means he probably is footy's version of Albert Einstein! For sure, some of the skills he produces on a football pitch defy the laws of physics!

CONFIDENCE	DRIBBLING	TRICKS	AGILITY	WEAK FOOT
92	86	94	85	73

23

LUIS DIAZ

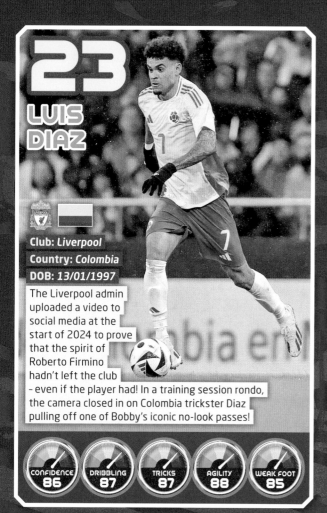

Club: *Liverpool*
Country: *Colombia*
DOB: *13/01/1997*

The Liverpool admin uploaded a video to social media at the start of 2024 to prove that the spirit of Roberto Firmino hadn't left the club – even if the player had! In a training session rondo, the camera closed in on Colombia trickster Diaz pulling off one of Bobby's iconic no-look passes!

CONFIDENCE	DRIBBLING	TRICKS	AGILITY	WEAK FOOT
86	87	87	88	85

22

JOAO FELIX

Club: *Chelsea*
Country: *Portugal*
DOB: *10/11/1999*

Playing for three different clubs in the space of two seasons isn't easy for anyone as it means you just can't settle in a side – and it definitely seemed to knock Felix's confidence! Saying that, we've still seen the Portuguese playmaker produce some savage pieces of skill during that period!

CONFIDENCE	DRIBBLING	TRICKS	AGILITY	WEAK FOOT
82	86	90	88	87

21

MOHAMED SALAH

TOP SKILL!
THE CUT

Club: *Liverpool*
Country: *Egypt*
DOB: *15/06/1992*

The Reds' record breaker set a whole host of new landmarks in 2023-24! As well as reaching 200 career league goals, he also hit his 200th goal for Liverpool in all comps, became the highest-scoring PL player for one club in Europe, and became the first star to score at least 20 goals in seven straight seasons for the Merseyside giants. Wow!

CONFIDENCE	DRIBBLING	TRICKS	AGILITY	WEAK FOOT
93	91	88	89	73

20
ANTONY

Club: *Man. United*
Country: *Brazil*
DOB: *24/02/2000*

Despite being born in the month of Valentine's Day, it's fair to say the Brazilian trickster still hasn't completely won over the hearts of Premier League fans! He certainly has the ability to make defenders blush with his skills and quick feet, but sometimes he picks the wrong moment to bust them out!

TOP SKILL!
THE 360 SPIN

CONFIDENCE
89

DRIBBLING
88

TRICKS
95

AGILITY
95

WEAK FOOT
73

MATCH! WOMEN SKILLERS

MAJRI

FACTFILE!

DOB: *25/01/1993*
Position: *Winger*
Club: *Lyon*
Country: *France*
Boot brand: *Nike*

DID YOU KNOW?

Amel perfected her technique as a kid using tennis balls and playing lots of beach footy!

FACTFILE!

DOB: *09/05/1995*
Position: *Winger*
Club: *Arsenal*
Country: *England*
Boot brand: *Nike*

DID YOU KNOW?

In 2022, Beth set a record for the most goals scored in a single season by an England player!

MEAD

WORDFIT

Fit the epic skillers who just missed out on this year's countdown into the giant grid!

Ait-Nouri	Firmino	Pedri
Barcola	Gnabry	Pedro
Camavinga	Gnonto	Raphinha
Cherki	Grealish	Solomon
Cunha	Guimaraes	Soule
Diallo	Guler	Trossard
Di Maria	Isak	Willian
Dybala	Ndiaye	Wirtz
Echeverri	Neres	Zinchenko
Fekir	Ounahi	Ziyech

WIRTZ

5 QUESTIONS ON...

ALEXIA PUTELLAS

1 Which Spanish side did she play for before joining Barcelona in 2012 - Levante, Atletico Madrid, Real Sociedad or Real Betis?

2 Which shirt number does she wear for Barcelona - No.9, No.11 or No.14?

3 What does her nickname "La Reina" translate to in English - The Reigning Champion, The Queen, The Legend or The Reindeer?

4 How many caps has Alexia won for Spain - more or less than 100?

5 True or False? She is the only player ever to win back-to-back Ballon d'Or Feminin awards!

SPOT THE BALL!

Mark where you think the ball should be in this cool action shot!

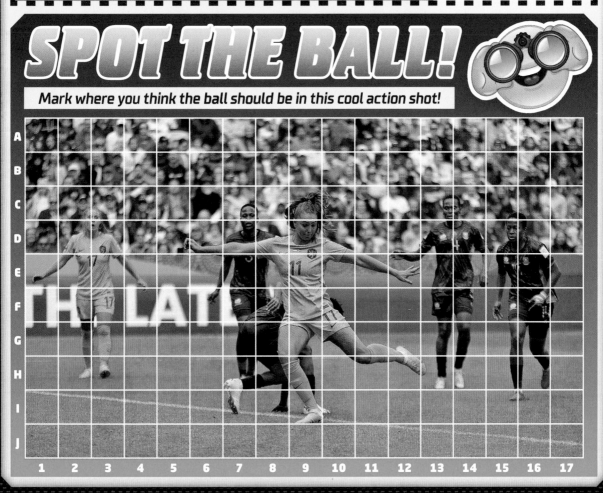

ANSWERS ON P60

TOP SKILL!
THE BODY SWERVE

19
SAVINHO

CONFIDENCE
90

DRIBBLING
93

TRICKS
90

AGILITY
87

WEAK FOOT
75

Club: Man. City
Country: Brazil
DOB: 10/04/2004

In his debut season in Spain in 2023-24, in a league that includes the likes of Vinicius Junior, Rodrygo and Raphinha, Savinho was the most successful dribbler...just let that sink in for a moment! The winger is going to be petrifying Prem full-backs for years to come!

18
KAORU MITOMA

Club: *Brighton*
Country: *Japan*
DOB: *20/05/1997*

Seagulls supporters must make really good deep-sea divers...not because they live on the coast, but because whenever Mitoma gets on the ball they all collectively hold their breath in anticipation of what he's going to do next! When the Japan winger gets one-on-one with a defender, you always back him to beat his marker!

TOP SKILL!
THE DRAG BACK

CONFIDENCE	DRIBBLING	TRICKS	AGILITY	WEAK FOOT
90	91	86	91	79

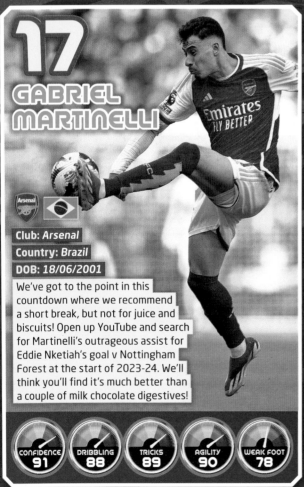

17
GABRIEL MARTINELLI

Club: *Arsenal*
Country: *Brazil*
DOB: *18/06/2001*

We've got to the point in this countdown where we recommend a short break, but not for juice and biscuits! Open up YouTube and search for Martinelli's outrageous assist for Eddie Nketiah's goal v Nottingham Forest at the start of 2023-24. We'll think you'll find it's much better than a couple of milk chocolate digestives!

CONFIDENCE	DRIBBLING	TRICKS	AGILITY	WEAK FOOT
91	88	89	90	78

16
MYKHAILO MUDRYK

Club: *Chelsea*
Country: *Ukraine*
DOB: *05/01/2001*

The Ukraine star became a national hero in 2024 after scoring the winner in the Euro 2024 play-off final v Iceland, which saw his country reach their third consecutive European Championship! He still has his critics in the Premier League but for pure tekkers alone, there aren't many better around!

CONFIDENCE	DRIBBLING	TRICKS	AGILITY	WEAK FOOT
82	87	94	88	88

15
JAMAL MUSIALA

TOP SKILL!
THE ONE-TOUCH TURN

Club: *Bayern Munich*
Country: *Germany*
DOB: *26/02/2003*

Whenever England supporters remember that Musiala played for The Three Lions up until the Under-21s, it's like a sucker punch to the gut - even though he was born in Germany! The way the ball glues to his feet when he dribbles reminds us that we need to stick some recent MATCH posters up on the wall!

CONFIDENCE	DRIBBLING	TRICKS	AGILITY	WEAK FOOT
88	90	85	93	86

14
LIONEL MESSI

Club: *Inter Miami*
Country: *Argentina*
DOB: *24/06/1987*

If you didn't see the clip of Messi chipping the ball over a Real Salt Lake defender who was lying on the ground in February 2024, before picking up the ball on the other side as if he were a cone, what rock were you hiding under? Even if you have seen it, it's definitely worth rewatching just for the LOLs. Leo's still got it!

CONFIDENCE	DRIBBLING	TRICKS	AGILITY	WEAK FOOT
99	90	82	87	83

13
JEREMY DOKU

Club: *Man. City*
Country: *Belgium*
DOB: *27/05/2002*

Doku is like one of those wind-up cars that, when you pull the string, go darting off unpredictably in all directions! He runs with the ball at such speed that defenders are terrified to make a tackle in case they give away a free-kick in a dangerous area - or worse, concede a penalty!

CONFIDENCE	DRIBBLING	TRICKS	AGILITY	WEAK FOOT
90	92	88	95	78

12
RAFAEL LEAO

Club: *Milan*
Country: *Portugal*
DOB: *10/06/1999*

Only a couple of players completed more dribbles in Serie A last season than Leao - including Argentina starlet Matias Soule, who looks set to make next year's skillers countdown - but the Milan forward's dribble success rate was better than both! He's like a tornado that can't be controlled once he gets going, with his crazy speed and unpredictability!

CONFIDENCE	DRIBBLING	TRICKS	AGILITY	WEAK FOOT
91	93	89	84	85

11
MOHAMMED KUDUS

Club: *West Ham*
Country: *Ghana*
DOB: *02/08/2000*

Watching Kudus play a game of football is like watching a Premier League -themed superhero film! There are epic battles that he looks destined to lose, where maybe he has run himself into a corner or a dead end, but it tends to have a happy ending because he more often than not dribbles his way out!

CONFIDENCE	DRIBBLING	TRICKS	AGILITY	WEAK FOOT
93	87	94	87	75

TOP SKILL!
THE DRAG BACK

10
RIYAD MAHREZ

Club: *Al Ahli*
Country: *Algeria*
DOB: *21/02/1991*

"Magical Mahrez and His Wand of a Left Foot" could be the name of a circus performance...and one that we'd definitely pay to see! Maybe his first trick could be pulling a bunny out of his shin pads, while standing on a spinning wheel. Easy peasy, lemon squeezy!

CONFIDENCE	DRIBBLING	TRICKS	AGILITY	WEAK FOOT
88	89	93	89	88

BAGGIO

Almost every football-loving child grows up idolising specific players, but not many go on to become as good as them! That was arguably the case for Baggio, who dreamt of following in the footsteps of Brazil legend Zico, known for his outstanding technical ability and incredible free-kicks. Despite suffering an almost career-ending injury when he was 18, Baggio did indeed become a set-piece specialist, while his dribbling, outrageously tight ball control and finesse finishing made him the all-round attacking package!

DID YOU KNOW?

BAGGIO WAS KNOWN AS IL DIVIN CODINO (THE DIVINE PONYTAIL), FOR THE HAIRSTYLE HE HAD FOR MOST OF HIS CAREER!

FACTPACK!

Full Name: *Roberto Baggio*

DOB: *18/02/1967*

Height: *5ft 9in*

Country: *Italy*

Caps: *56*

Goals: *27*

CAREER LEAGUE STATS

Date	Club	Games	Goals
1982-1985	Vicenza	36	13
1985-1990	Fiorentina	94	39
1990-1995	Juventus	141	78
1995-1997	Milan	51	12
1997-1998	Bologna	30	22
1998-2000	Inter	41	9
2000-2004	Brescia	95	45

CONFIDENCE 97

DRIBBLING 98

TRICKS 96

AGILITY 88

WEAK FOOT 88

SHOWREEL!

Scan the QR code to watch some of his best bits!

MATCH! WOMEN SKILLERS

CUTHBERT

FACTFILE!

DOB: 19/07/1998
Position: Midfielder
Club: Chelsea
Country: Scotland
Boot brand: Nike

DID YOU KNOW?

Erin was voted Scotland Women's Player of the Year for the third time in December 2023!

GEYSE

FACTFILE!

DOB: 27/03/1998

Position: Forward

Club: Man. United

Country: Brazil

Boot brand: adidas

DID YOU KNOW?

No player made more progressive ball carries in the Women's Super League in 2023-24 than Geyse!

TOP SKILL!
THE HOCUS POCUS

9
WILFRIED ZAHA

Club: *Lyon*

Country: *Ivory Coast*

DOB: *10/11/1992*

There has been a Zaha-shaped hole in the Premier League since the forward's move to Galatasaray in 2023, but MATCH made sure to keep on top of his performances in Turkey! He cooked over there, but it was the footy equivalent of tasty Turkish Delight rather than a delicious English breakfast. He's on loan at Lyon for 2024-25!

CONFIDENCE
94

DRIBBLING
88

TRICKS
95

AGILITY
88

WEAK FOOT
81

8
RODRYGO

TOP SKILL!
LA CROQUETA

Club: *Real Madrid*
Country: *Brazil*
DOB: *09/01/2001*

Brazilian club Santos have developed some of the most skilful footballers of all time from their academy, including all-time legends Pele, Edu, Neymar and now Rodrygo! His link-up with club and international team-mate Vinicius Jr. is telepathic – it's like they can read each others' minds!

CONFIDENCE	DRIBBLING	TRICKS	AGILITY	WEAK FOOT
89	89	93	89	87

TOP SKILL!
THE SCOOP TURN

7
KHVICHA KVARATSKHELIA

Club: *Napoli*
Country: *Georgia*
DOB: *12/02/2001*

Even though Napoli had a stinker of a 2023-24 season, "Kvaradona" still completed more successful dribbles than any other player in Italy last campaign, and was the Champions League's best dribbler until Napoli were knocked out! The Georgia talisman has got the flair to tear apart any defence!

CONFIDENCE	DRIBBLING	TRICKS	AGILITY	WEAK FOOT
90	95	86	91	89

6
OUSMANE DEMBELE

Club: *PSG*
Country: *France*
DOB: *15/05/1997*

When Dembele was asked in an interview if he was left or right footed, he simply replied, "both"! That's probably his biggest standout feature, because even though he appears to use his left foot more when dribbling, he prefers taking penalties with his right foot. Try figuring that riddle out!

CONFIDENCE	DRIBBLING	TRICKS	AGILITY	WEAK FOOT
89	90	94	90	95

5
ALLAN SAINT-MAXIMIN

Club: *Fenerbahce*
Country: *France*
DOB: *12/03/1997*

We miss seeing Saint-Maximin ripping up the Premier League every week with his chaotic fast feet, electric dribbling and mind-boggling skills! The Fenerbahce ace, on loan from Al Ahli, made the Saudi Pro League look like when you set your fave video game to extra easy mode – it's "Mission Complete" every single time!

CONFIDENCE	DRIBBLING	TRICKS	AGILITY	WEAK FOOT
93	93	95	92	86

4

LUCAS PAQUETA

DID YOU KNOW?

IN 2023-24, PAQUETA BECAME ONLY THE SECOND BRAZILIAN IN HISTORY TO ASSIST THREE GOALS IN A SINGLE PREMIER LEAGUE GAME!

Club: *West Ham*

Country: *Brazil*

DOB: *27/08/1997*

Every year, we like to make a big song and dance about the jaw-dropping skillers who have impressed us the most! Not literally, obviously...although if we did it'd have to be a Brazil's Got Talent level routine to match Paqueta's moves on the footy pitch!

CONFIDENCE 93

DRIBBLING 87

TRICKS 97

AGILITY 90

WEAK FOOT 92

BRAIN-BUSTER!

How well do you know some of footy's best tricksters?

1. Who was the first La Liga player to complete 80 dribbles in 2023-24 – Savio, Vinicius Junior or Rodrygo?

87
CAM

Magull

PAC 81 SHO 74 PAS 84 DRI 86 DEF 57 PHY 68

2. How many skill stars did Germany winger Lina Magull have on epic footy videogame EA FC 24?

3. What cool boot brand did footy legend Ronaldinho used to wear?

4. True or False? USA trickster Rose Lavelle spent a season in the Women's Super League with Arsenal!

5. Which UK nation did iconic skiller George Best used to play for?

6. Which of these isn't a famous skill move – The Elastico, The Nutcracker or The Rainbow Flick?

7. Football freestylers Jeremy Lynch and Billy Wingrove were otherwise known by which name?

8. Which Bayern skiller has more followers on Instagram – Leroy Sane or Kingsley Coman?

9. How many caps has trickster Debinha won for Brazil women's team – more or less than 100?

10. True or False? The home changing room at the Maracana is named after legendary Brazil skiller Garrincha!

1 ....
2 ....
3 ....
4 ....
5 ....
6 ....
7 ....
8 ....
9 ....
10 ....

FACE IN THE CROWD

Can you spot the ten jaw-dropping skillers in this crowd? They're all in there somewhere!

Ronaldo

Neto

Palmer

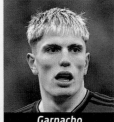

Garnacho

Depay

Leao

Musiala

Eze

Foden

Odegaard

ANSWERS ON PAGE 60

FOWLER

FACTFILE!

DOB: *14/02/2003*
Position: *Forward*
Club: *Man. City*
Country: *Australia*
Boot brand: *adidas*

DID YOU KNOW?

Mary was named in the Matildas squad for the Paris 2024 Olympics - her second Olympic Games selection!

FACTFILE!

DOB: 22/02/2005
Position: Forward
Club: Real Madrid
Country: Colombia
Boot brand: adidas

DID YOU KNOW?

Linda was handed the 2023 Golden Girl award as the best female Under-21 footballer playing in Europe!

CAICEDO

3 NEYMAR

TOP SKILL!
THE RAINBOW FLICK

Club: Al Hilal
Country: Brazil
DOB: 05/02/1992

Neymar is football's great entertainer but injuries are the pantomime villain! His move to Al Hilal felt like a new beginning after a stop-start spell in France with PSG, but a serious knee injury meant he played just three games in his first season in Saudi Arabia. We're crossing our fingers he can have more luck, because he's a one-of-a-kind talent!

CONFIDENCE 94

DRIBBLING 94

TRICKS 98

AGILITY 90

WEAK FOOT 89

2
VINICIUS JUNIOR

TOP SKILL!
THE SCOOP TURN FAKE

DID YOU KNOW?

VINI JR. SCORED EIGHT GOALS IN HIS FIRST 11 GAMES AGAINST VALENCIA — MORE THAN ANY OTHER SIDE!

Club: *Real Madrid*
Country: *Brazil*
DOB: *12/07/2000*

Vinicius' reign as the No.1 skiller on the planet lasted just one term, but he'll be pumped to return to top spot next year! Part of his problem in 2023-24 was having to start more centrally, so he found himself with his back to goal rather than squaring up to his man on the wing. That looks to have changed this campaign, though!

CONFIDENCE
96

DRIBBLING
95

TRICKS
96

AGILITY
96

WEAK FOOT
88

TURN THE PAGE TO FIND OUT WHO'S OUR NO.1!

1

KYLIAN MBAPPE

Club: *Real Madrid*
Country: *France*
DOB: *20/12/1998*

There's a new name for the history books! Mbappe has become just the third player to be awarded MATCH's world-famous "Best Skiller on the Planet" prize! In what was a fitting end to his glittering PSG spell, Kylian won yet another Ligue 1 top scorer prize before making the move to Real Madrid for the next chapter in his top-quality career!

TOP SKILL!
THE FAKE RABONA

DID YOU KNOW?
BY JOINING LOS BLANCOS ON A HUGE CONTRACT, MBAPPE BECAME REAL MADRID'S HIGHEST-PAID PLAYER IN HISTORY. WOW!

CONFIDENCE
99

DRIBBLING
95

TRICKS
95

AGILITY
94

WEAK FOOT
89

STAT ATTACK!

KYLIAN MBAPPE

We check out some of the sickest stats and facts from the new king of skills!

220+

In his final three seasons at PSG, he completed over 220 league dribbles. Wow!

6

He's the only player in Ligue 1 history to earn as many as six top scorer prizes – winning his sixth in a row in 2023-24!

10

Mbappe is the first player to score at least one goal in ten consecutive games started at home in Champions League history!

111

In the 2021-22 season, he was the only player in the French league to complete over 100 dribbles!

2

Mbappe is the youngest Champions League goalscorer for two different clubs – Monaco and PSG!

59

No Ligue 1 player had more shots on target than Mbappe in 2023-24!

1

He's the only player to finish as both top scorer and assist provider in the same Ligue 1 season!

6

He was directly involved in six goals in France's biggest-ever win – their 14-0 thrashing of Gibraltar in November 2023!

256

Mbappe left PSG as their all-time record goalscorer, with 256 net-busters in just 308 games. Lethal!

3

He scored three goals in five Champions League games against Real Madrid as a PSG player!

4

No player has scored more goals in World Cup finals than Mbappe's four!

COMPETITION

Don't agree with MATCH's top five tricksters? Now's the chance to have your say!

RONALDO
Al Nassr & Portugal

MESSI
Inter Miami & Argentina

MBAPPE
Real Madrid & France

WIN!
RIG 300 PRO COSMIC PURPLE GAMING HEADSET!

Just pick your five favourite footy skillers, send it to MATCH and you could win this **RIG 300 PRO Cosmic Purple Gaming Headset** for PlayStation!

Visit **nacongaming.com** for more epic gaming accessories!

PICK YOUR TOP 5 FAVE SKILLERS!

YAMAL
Barcelona & Spain

SIMONS
RB Leipzig & Netherlands

DIAZ
Liverpool & Colombia

For the chance to win a **RIG 300 PRO Cosmic Purple Gaming Headset**, just write down your five favourite skillers, fill out your contact details and email a photograph of this page to: **match.magazine@kelsey.co.uk** **Closing date: January 31, 2025**. One lucky winner will be picked at random. What are you waiting for?

1.

2.

3.

4.

5.

NAME:

ADDRESS:

NUMBER:

EMAIL:

IBRAHIMOVIC

FACTPACK!

Full Name: *Zlatan Ibrahimovic*

DOB: *03/10/1981*

Height: *6ft 5in*

Country: *Sweden*

Caps: *122*

Goals: *62*

"Arsene Wenger asked me to have a trial with Arsenal when I was 17. I turned it down. Zlatan doesn't do auditions." That quote pretty much sums up Ibrahimovic! He was a bold and uber confident player, who wasn't afraid to try the unimaginable – just like his 35-yard bicycle kick for Sweden against England back in 2013, which was later awarded the Puskas Award for goal of the year. That was one of 62 goals for his country, which remains Sweden's all-time record – and one that may never be broken!

DID YOU KNOW?

ZLATAN IS THE ONLY PLAYER TO SCORE IN THE CHAMPIONS LEAGUE FOR SIX DIFFERENT TEAMS – AJAX, JUVENTUS, INTER, BARCELONA, MILAN AND PSG!

CAREER LEAGUE STATS

Date	Club	Games	Goals
1999-2001	Malmo	40	16
2001-2004	Ajax	74	35
2004-2006	Juventus	70	23
2006-2009	Inter	88	57
2009-2011	Barcelona	29	16
2010-2012	Milan	61	42
2012-2016	PSG	122	113
2016-2018	Man. United	33	17
2018-2019	LA Galaxy	56	52
2020-2023	Milan	64	34

TOP SKILL!
POPCORN FLICK

SHOWREEL!

Scan the QR code to watch some of his best bits!

CONFIDENCE
100

DRIBBLING
84

TRICKS
96

AGILITY
85

WEAK FOOT
86

CROSSWORD

Use the clues below to fill in MATCH's tricky crossword!

ACROSS

2. Boot silo from adidas that trick machine Paulo Dybala wears! (4)

4. Skill move often used by Cristiano Ronaldo! (4)

5. The number of times Lionel Messi has won the Ballon d'Or! (5)

6. Finish the skill move... Around The _ _ _ _ _! (5)

7. Shirt number that Vinicius Junior wears for Real Madrid! (5)

9. Foot that retired Spain and Man. City icon David Silva preferred to use! (4)

12. Country skiller Dimitar Berbatov played for! (8)

13. MATCH's No.1 skiller in the 2021 Annual! (6)

16. Prem side that Steve McManaman played the most games for! (9)

17. Angel Di Maria's funny food-related nickname! (6)

18. Zinedine Zidane's famous nickname! (5)

DOWN

1. Month that Arsenal and England wing wizard Bukayo Saka was born! (9)

3. Finish the Skill Move... The McGeady _ _ _ _! (4)

4. Women skiller who scored England's Euro 2022 final winner! (5,5)

8. European country that Hakim Ziyech played youth football for before switching to Morocco! (11)

10. Legendary Portugal winger who played for both Real Madrid and Barcelona! (4,4)

11. Brazil Women's all-time top goalscorer and jaw-dropping skiller! (5)

13. Italian club Diego Maradona won the Serie A title with! (6)

14. Legendary skiller Edson Arantes do Nascimento – AKA...! (4)

15. World champion freestyler whose surname is Cooke! (3)

WHO STARTED WHERE?

Have a go at matching the trick machines with the clubs they started their careers at!

1 PEDRO NETO	2 WILFRIED ZAHA	3 KINGSLEY COMAN	4 RIYAD MAHREZ	5 VINICIUS JUNIOR	6 RODRYGO

A SANTOS	B FLAMENGO	C BRAGA	D PSG	E QUIMPER	F CRYSTAL PALACE

ODD ONE OUT!

Jeremy Doku

Hakim Ziyech

Christopher Nkunku

Rafael Leao

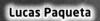
Lucas Paqueta

Which of these sick skillers has NEVER played in France's Ligue 1?

Julian Draxler

ANSWERS ON PAGE 60

Wordsearch P20

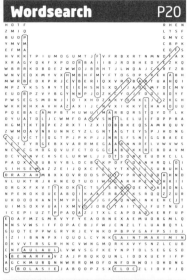

Footy Mis-Match P21

Wordfit P30

Alexia Putellas Quiz P31

1. Levante;
2. No.11;
3. The Queen;
4. More than 100;
5. True.

Spot The Ball P31

I 11.

Brain-Buster P44

1. Savio; 2. Five stars;
3. Nike; 4. False – she spent a season at Man. City; 5. Northern Ireland; 6. The Nutcracker;
7. The F2; 8. Leroy Sane;
9. More than 100; 10. True.

Face In The Crowd P45

Crossword P58

Who Started Where? P59

1C; 2F; 3D; 4E; 5B; 6A.

Odd One Out P59

Hakim Ziyech.

LOVE MATCH?
GET IT DELIVERED EVERY FORTNIGHT!

SAVING 57%
ON THE FULL SHOP PRICE!*
ONLY £39.99 FOR 13 ISSUES!

PACKED EVERY ISSUE WITH...

★ Red-hot gear

★ News & gossip

★ Stats & quizzes

★ Massive stars

★ Posters & pics

& loads more!